BROUGHT TO LIGHT

Jem Poster originally worked as an archaeologist, surveying and excavating a range of sites on behalf of the Inspectorate of Ancient Monuments, before taking up an administrative post with Cambridge University's Board of Continuing Education. Since 1993 he has been Lecturer in Literature with Oxford University's Department for Continuing Education and a Fellow of Kellogg College; since 1998 he has been director of the department's Diploma in Creative Writing.

His other publications include a selection of George Crabbe's poetry, a study of the poetry of the 1930s and articles on modern poetry and fiction. His pamphlet, *By Some Other Route*, was published by the Mandeville Press in 1993. *Brought to Light* (Bloodaxe Books, 2001) is his first book-length collection.

Jem Poster

BROUGHT TO LIGHT

BLOODAXE BOOKS

ISBN: 1 85224 568 9

First published 2001 by
Bloodaxe Books Ltd,
Highgreen,
Tarset,
Northumberland NE48 1RP.

Bloodaxe Books Ltd acknowledges
the financial assistance of Northern Arts.

Cover printing by J. Thomson Colour Printers Ltd, Glasgow.

Printed in Great Britain by
Cromwell Press Ltd, Trowbridge, Wiltshire.

For Tom and Tobi

Acknowledgements

Acknowledgements are due to the editors of the following publications, in which some of these poems first appeared: *Acumen, Agenda, Arvon Foundation International Poetry Competition Anthology, Bucket of Tongues, The Cambridge Review, London Magazine, New Welsh Review, Orbis, Oxford Magazine, Oxford Poetry, PN Review, Poetry London, The Rialto* and *Sycamore Review.* Ten of the poems appeared, some in slightly different form, in a Mandeville Press pamphlet, *By Some Other Route* (1993).

'The Collectors' was awarded first prize in the 1995 Cardiff International Poetry Competition and 'Incident' was awarded fourth prize in the same competition in 1999. 'Conjuror' won fourth prize in the Peterloo Poets Open Poetry Competition in 1997 and 'Pastoral' won first prize in the same competition in 2001. 'Dealing with Circe' was shortlisted in the Arvon Foundation International Poetry Competition in 2000.

Contents

There

It's happening, like almost everything,
in another world: the green
larva unclasps its feet, drops from the ribbed
leaf in the unseen canopy and swings
earthward on a shining thread to fall
just where you might be standing if you'd left
the path ten seconds earlier, losing itself
in the untrodden leafmould; and you can't come at it,
that dark translation, the skin split to disclose
to no one's eyes the hardening
armature and what would be the gleam
of its burnished contours if – but the blackbird's shuffling
the litter somewhere else and you'll not pass
that way again – the thing were brought to light.

The Collectors

I can't get them out of my mind, the Victorian collectors
out at the margins of the recorded world, equipped
with rifles, nets and notebooks, taking the measure
of their own astonishment. I see them moving
efficiently up nameless tributaries, pressing
into the hinterlands, the preposterous globe
shrinking beneath their bootsoles.

                              Two scenes, precise
as steel engravings. This: a figure seated
at a makeshift table; yellow light
spilt from an oil-lamp; a canvas roll
of surgical instruments. He reaches into the mouth
of a satchel at his feet, draws out
an iridescent body; leans over it with a lover's
elaborate solicitude, purses his lips and blows. The down
parts along the breastbone.
And now he's taking up the scalpel, guiding
the blade from throat to vent. It seems so easy,
skin and bright feathers lifted like a gown,
the flesh exposed.
                     And this: he's lying
among the twisted blankets on the floor
of an unstable lean-to, shaking with fever, blood
crusted beneath his nails. Does he know it's ending,
the long imperial dream, the unsustainable
illusion of control? His staring eyes
give nothing away.

                    Beyond the threshold
the intolerable sunlight, the mound of carcasses
clouded with flies. And further, much further,
perhaps already out of reach, the shaded
drawing-rooms dusted by obedient hands; the glass
domes and cabinets, the cluttered
tableaux. Static frenzy of wings; an age's
immoderate longings flocking home to roost.

Incident

Whether they were praying as the boat slewed round
scraping the harbour wall, the wet rope slipping
from its mooring-ring, I couldn't say. Their pinched
lips moved, though not in unison, and certainly
their hands were clasped before them, fingers locked,
shining with spray. I hardly care. What matters
is my own inaction. I might have grasped the line
or, failing that, kicked off my boots and plunged
into the ruffled water, seized the prow
and swung them back to safety.

                Risky? Yes, but better death,
I sometimes think, than this endless inquisition,
the tears I can't quite shed, the sense of something
betrayed and still unmourned. As it was, I stood
on the slimy cobbles and watched them go, my eyes
smarting with salt and strain; and as they crossed
the harbour-bar, a cry went up, a soft
keening which faded as they drifted out
between the rafts of kelp, faces uplifted
and swivelled landward. That's how I see them now,
helpless, abandoned to the swell, their small
unworldly features blurred by distance, gazing
perhaps at me, perhaps towards the shrouded
mountains at my back. And if I look
for some consolatory gesture, an arm upraised
in blessing, it might be, or farewell, I find
not the faintest hint; only the fragile craft
dwindling to nothing; and the indifferent sea.

Veteran

This is his refuge, a ten-pole plot
beside the railway track. Beet, parsnips, leeks
stiff in their weedless rows. He's digging in
the withering beanstalks, slicing through topsoil,
roots, earthworms, larvae. The broken loam
steams in the sunlight. His shoulders ease, he moves
with the old assurance. And here it comes again,
like the metallic whisper thrilling down the line
as the train approaches, that pervasive tremor
of anticipation. Salt on his lips, the landing-craft
riding the swell, spray sweeping
its crowded deck. Poise
and thrust, arc of the body's blind
trajectory. It's on him now, the thunder
of the InterCity; that and the familiar
congestion as his heartbeats quicken
and stutter. His boots are heavy, his palms
slick with sweat; he stumbles
on the chopped earth, in the clucking shingle, back
where the breakers seethe and roar. There in the darkness
a voice begins to scream and won't be hushed.

Again

But if I start with that – the way he breaks
from the coppice, head down, one arm crooked forward, shielding
his face from the stinging twigs – I hit the thing
off-centre. Yes, that's what I best remember,
that and his headlong flight across the blanched
meadows to the garden where his mother
in thornproof gloves, dead-heading the roses, turns
at the click of the gate-latch; but there's something
I've not accounted for, a faint vibration
subtle but too insistent to ignore.
                             I'll
start again. He's standing at the muffled
heart of the coppice where the water gathers
in a sullen pool. Honeysuckle and decay; the smell
of his own prickling skin. Above, the leaves
whisper and stir incessantly, but here
nothing moves; unless perhaps a breath
or tremor wrinkling the filmy surface –
                                  Out,
out and running. This time I feel the uneven
ground beneath his plimsolls, feel the barbs
snag the shoulder of his T-shirt as he ducks
under the shivering wire. The blood
sings in his head; and as the gate slams back
on its rusted hinges I see the garden's long
perspective blur and slide.
                         A flurry
of unfocussed movement; the gloves flung down
beside the rocking trug, a hand outstretched
to steady him as he reels. He's gasping
something his mother strains to catch but can't
make head or tail of. He'll have to start again.

Listening

Always from some other room, intermittent,
unsourceable, just loud enough
to rouse me; and every night the same
quick surge of blood in my chest and throat, the panicky
scanning of darkness, all my bearings gone
in a house she'll never visit. I tell myself
it can't be her, it can't be
her, but by then of course I'm wide awake
and listening. And although she said she couldn't
envisage – no, not her, but someone's fucking
someone. I hear them at it through the long
implacable hours – the muted
chime of an earring as she slips the hook
free of the reddened lobe; a hangnail snagging
the loose thread of a buttonhole; the hush
of fabric drawn from scented shoulders, sliding
to the floor. And they're subtle: no cries or moans but
if I hold my breath I hear the whisper
of skin on skin, the shining down brushed upward
in the hollow of her back; the impeded
passage of air through lips she's easing open
under the pressure of his tongue.
                                        So I might go down,
rake up the embers and squat beside the hearth,
my hands outstretched for warmth; or huddle
in the angle of the chimney-breast, embracing
my own hunched shoulders. No refuge there
or anywhere. This morning I stormed
from the house at daybreak, stumbling through the meadows
to the river's edge; knelt and plunged my face
in the swollen torrent until my cheekbones ached and
my eyelids stung. And it might have been the thin
voice of the alders singing in the wind or
the sigh of the grasses; but as I raised my head
I thought I could just make out behind the roar
of the battering waters something like the *ah*
spilt from the mouths of lovers in the unguarded
instant before they drift apart and fall
from each other's arms to face the dark alone.

14

Now

The bar, as the bulletins will tell us later,
packed with the usual lunchtime crowds. The device
already detonated, the fragments flying outward
from their hidden centre; and in this split
second the girl with the razor-cut hair and delicate
untroubled features is draining her glass, her eyes
fixed on her lover's face, a sliver
of lime against her palate, her lifted tongue
testing the fruit's sour flesh. And because the air
is filled with music, because the sunlight's falling
on her shoulder like a blessing – the glass's stem
intact between her fingers – she starts to smile.

Visiting
(i.m. Harold and Beatrice Hoyle)

I

I'm at my daughter's apron-strings. I prattle
incontinently as she sweeps the dust
clear of the threshold; or watch her stooping
to scrub the dented churns, sensing too late (chapped
knuckles blanching suddenly) her cold
inhibited anger.
            I turn away and wander
out through the gateway, drifting, dazed by light,
across the rising grassland, climbing until
the blood throbs at my temples and the familiar
tightness around my chest, the hint of nausea,
bring me to a standstill.
                The plovers scream and wheel,
mocking my backward glance. Below, the farm
smart as a painted toy; my daughter clattering
unseen behind the barn, the churns upended
on the slatted trestle. And now my grandchild saunters
into the yard, squats down, her bare feet splayed
on the hot cobbles, lifts her face
easily to the sun; and I'm shaken
by a febrile tenderness, burn to set my hand
to the long curve of her throat, to know
through palm and fingertips that cool
distressing fluency.

              Beyond the ridge, the slow
descent to the shining estuary through meadows
hazed with the grasses' arching flowerheads, seamed
by the ranker green of silted cuts which run
away to uncertain distance. I pick my way
stiffly between the tussocks, find at last
my path crossed by a deeper channel; brace
my aching legs, step down into the dark
foetor of growth and rot, pressing between
dense umbels, rasping leaves, the spongy ground
giving beneath me.

My extended hand
closes on nothing and I stumble,
cracking the hollow stems, the pollen streaming
out on the shimmering air. The world
grows treacherous as a childhood dream. I sprawl
full-length among the shifting roots and cry.

II

I step inside, breathing again the tainted
heat of the corridor, the subtle
ammoniac presence gathering in my throat
like a remembered grief. There, where the stark
perspective ends, an orderly hooks back
the heavy doors, hauls in a trolley, shoulders
rounded with effort.
                                I enter to the clatter
of crockery, the unfocused murmur
of female voices. The nurse looks up, a smile
half-forming on her lips; but I'm scanning
the faces behind her – the mumbling jaws, the bleak
abstracted gazes of the lost.

                                I find her
seated at the window, staring blankly
across the parching lawns. Someone has cropped
her thinning hair so close I see the knobbed
contours of bone behind the ears. Her gown
rides upward to her thighs, her restless fingers
pluck at the hem; the urgent, saddening phrases
break from her lips like spittle.
                                Now she turns,
holds out her wasted hand; and I'm passing
back down the long sour corridor to the first
of all the rented rooms we loved in. Rain
on the summer garden and the curtains stirring
to the slow indraught; the brush
of loosened satin, catch of her breath; that hand
reaching through the fragrant dark to guide me home.

Taking Leave

Things have changed since my arrival. First
I mislaid my watch; and though it occurred to me
I shouldn't need it here, I sat and cried
as if for a friend or lover. Since then I've lost
diary, address-book, the little clutch of keys
on its silver ring; and other things besides,
too small to be worth remembering. Now I let the days
fall into place around me, rest my eyes
on neutral distance, on the unexplored
acres of parkland, the lake, the forest's
encroaching shadow. I scarcely recognise
the interchangeable faces of the past,
the frail imploring hands. I watch them fade
caring less and less, though sensitive to the slightest
shift or tremor – a freshening of the breeze,
stirrings in the leafmould, the whisper of dried
pods in the shrubbery; move at ease
between the untended borders, belly and breasts
darkening beneath the tatters of my blouse,
the bracelet of blond skin around my wrist
shading to nothing. I'm growing used
to these quiet effacements. Sometimes I test
on tongue and palate the currency of such words
as I have not forgotten: husband, children, rose,
marigold, aster, willowherb... The list
is dwindling. When there's nothing left to lose
I shall move on, follow the drifting seeds
across the lawns, down the long avenues
to find myself among the nameless trees.

Archangel

My children have never seen it. It was common here
I tell them, twitching aside the brambles, scanning
the trampled clearing. Sweet-wrappers, cans,
the usual debris.

                    Perhaps it was somewhere else
I stood that morning, shorts unbuttoned, pissing
into the beaded grasses as the sun
struck through the rainclouds and the clustered florets
glowed yellow as lemons. A stirring
of hidden life around me; a scent of
is it mint? I can't
quite catch it, but it's there, inseparable
from urine and archangel, from the golden light
streaming between the beeches.

                    I'm on my knees, I'm searching
for a shoot, a stem, a leaf, for whatever rises
fragrant, ammoniac from the moistened earth.

Away

I *Missing*

Missing you still; this morning
at the field's brown margin, listening to the dry
whisper of uncropped maize; or hearing
as the comb snags in his tangled hair the cry
of the serious child who took your place but leaves
intact some unimaginable space.

And did I dream your body borne
from the ward on a covered tray? The image
refuses to be drawn, but you're there, a cold
uncradled darkness, an enduring
vacancy; something, I mean, cries out
for shaping but will not, although we reach
back through the years for knowledge of the seed
of this vast unfulfilment, come to hand.

II *Driving*

The engine overheats. I ignore the warning
flickering on the dashboard as we climb
clear of the valley. Less easy to ignore
the bickering kids, your stifled
anger as you guide us through the web
of dusty lanes, one finger tracing
our progress on the map. We know
exactly where we are, you insist; no point
stopping to ask.

These scattered hamlets
glimpsed as we pass. A stand
of limes about a shaded yard; the luminous
foliage of trellised vines; two farm-cats
sprawled in the hazy sunlight like a couple
satiate with loving, watching the world go by.

III *Church*

Blue stars of chicory against the cream
stone of the porch, the heavy doors
thrown wide.

            An unsourced murmur
of prayer or conversation. The nave
flooded with chalky light; a nun
scouring the hollowed flags, head bowed
over her humbling task. On either side
these incongruous plaster figures: the arrested
gestures, uplifted gazes and the stiff
fall of pastel robes to feet
firm on their solid plinths. An offering
of artificial roses and all around the little
votive plaques: *Merci ô Marie*. O mother,
the answerings; these pale walls washed by voices;
inalienable congregations, another tongue.

IV *Name This Insect*

This book was mine. Today I've watched you turning
the thumbed plates, savouring the names; or stalking
the shimmering meadows. For myself, I remember
the longing for possession; that and the dusty
frenzy against the net's coarse mesh, the dull
inexplicable disappointments. What I wanted then,
scanning the pages, the fields, the woodland rides,
I can't imagine.

            And now you're lapsing
quietly into sleep, leaving me at ease
on the darkening terrace. A breath of wind
stirring the walnut leaves, the crickets'
inarticulate stridency; and somewhere out there the vivid
Mazarine Blues, the Clouded Yellows, wings
folded at last among the leaning grasses.

21

V *Still*

I'm ready to go; but you're out with the children
at the meadow's edge, reaching into the brambles,
absorbed, unhurried. As I approach
you turn, one arm outstretched, the berries
cupped in your palm. The children take,
eat.

    Leaving, as we must,
threading the narrow lanes, wheels brushing
the yellowing bracken. In my mirror
the village, folded among the lenient hills,
dropping behind us. Still, of course, the sunlight
warming the stonework; peaches and melons piled
in the crammed market-place. But also the hush
of shuttered rooms, the chill
of untenanted space; all we have left unspoken.

Child

This morning, hunting through the meadows
for the unfamiliar: shield-bugs
clustered on the fennel-flowers, the elegant
parasitic wasps, the mantids
at their fierce devotions. Your hands
trembling; with excitement, yes, but –
                                    You ignored
my questions. Touched by your nervous
reticence, I stooped and held you
a moment in my arms. You smiled,
reassured, I thought. But tonight you ask me
to see you safely to your room, to leave
the lamp on while you sleep.
                            In the still hours
your cry rings out. I'm helpless, drifting
through a shadowed landscape, bewildered by your voice's
unplaceable resonance. I kneel and push aside
curtains of rasping foliage: something squirms
beneath a litter of rotting stems.
                                I'm on my feet
and running. I meet you in the half-light
of the long corridor; your eyes are glazed, your
round face blank with panic.
                            Put
your arms around me, hold me tight.

Leadership Training

The organisation was superb. The delegates
were – to a man – my type, and from the outset
I wanted to be part of things. The firm
was paying, and though the schedule seemed
perhaps a little light, I soon
stopped fretting about such details. Each afternoon,
tea from bone china, tiny fragrant cakes
melting like honey on the tongue. As it grew dark
candles were lit, the curtains drawn, the tables
laid by discreet hands.
                              It's impossible
to do justice to those dinners: seafood,
sometimes in bubbling stews, more often fried
in a yellow batter; quail
served by the dozen, wafers of veal
flaking beneath the knife; the thick
tranches of beef and lamb, the aromatic
sauces and sorbets. And then the women
moving from table to table, table to bed, benign,
endlessly compliant, though none of them spoke
or smiled. The jokes
were wild beyond belief. Once you started laughing
you couldn't stop. One morning,
entering for breakfast a little late, I found,
palm upward in the muffin-dish, a hand
severed at the wrist. Of course I was stunned
but saw the funny side.
                              Sometimes it crossed my mind
it might be best to leave; but then
what about my colleagues? How could I let them down?

Towards Dawn

I

Is it a fox? Through heavy undergrowth
I catch a glimpse of reddish fur, of glistening
skin drawn back from nacreous teeth. Advancing,
I try to flush it out, thrusting my arms
against the resistant scrub until something gives
and I press inward
grazing rough flanks. There in the darkness
I raise my muzzle to the sky and scream.

II

They're pulling down the temples. From the terrace
I watch the falling masonry, the tremors
shaking my own frame, intimations
of irremediable loss. Even the beeches,
whose smooth grey boles themselves resemble columns
of weathered stone, are threatened, As I watch
someone comes driving hard along the margin
of the placid lake; I see the spray thrown up
by the car's thick tyres. And all around
the orange fires of demolition, smoke
rising in plumes, pale flakes of drifting ash.

III

This is your dream, not mine; but I see you
now, as the windows whiten, walking between
autumnal borders in a walled garden. Silence; a taut
expectancy; and sunlight
subdued, you write, *and fading*, shed on paths
and lawns, on abraded stonework. A premonition
of frost on the lapsing air.

For you, there are always doorways. This,
set in the surrounding wall, is hung with foliage
which you part. I see
the bolt slide from its socket; and you,
your arms outstretched before you, opening –
but here your letter grows confused – yes, opening
the door on unimaginable light.

Story

A fairytale childhood
showered with blessings; your
translucent beauty, the
laughter, the cleverness.
What more were you after
twisting the tourniquet,
probing the scarred
veins of your forearm?
And how did it start?
Only a needleprick
but you must have foreseen it –
you and your destiny
coldly converging;
the terror, the ecstasy,
blood on the coverlet,
rain on the streets and you
sleeping forever.

Mackerel

The heat that year was stifling. My father led me
across the hills on walks which petered out
in trackless silence. What I wanted
was unspeakable and somewhere else. At dusk
I cruised the streets and seafront where the girls
stalked in pairs or clustered in the doorways
of the brash arcades. I inhaled
perfume and cigarette-smoke, intimations
of unfathomable risk, passed on, devising
improbable encounters; watched the yachts
strain gently at their moorings.

From the sea
the town seemed insubstantial. Hunched
in the stern, I saw it gather itself, receding
into luminous distance; paid out the line.
The signal
was almost imperceptible: a twitch, the hook
lodged fast; a deepening tremor. Hand
over feverish hand, the rising blood
congesting chest and throat. A gleam,
clouded at first but brightening; the fish
dragged to the light, its side and belly breaking
the troubled surface.

I lean into the spray
breathless, salt-mouthed. I
have it now: the reddened gills, the thrilling
smell on my palms; the frenzied shimmering body
drumming the boards, impatient to be gone.

Terms of Reference

I'd marked the route in pencil, tracing the footpath's
ascent through the clustered contours, noting
significant landmarks: the reservoir, the falls, a wedge
of woodland. Clear enough; but the path itself,
a wavering thread encroached upon by scrub,
proved almost indecipherable. I struggled upward
breathless, bewildered, to find myself at last
on an outcrop high above the valley.
                                    Nothing
had prepared me for that giddy confrontation
with sunlit space. I might have stepped
clear into vacancy, but stumbled backward
to safer ground. Crouched in a hollow, shaken
by my own unruly heartbeats, I cast around
for anchorage: thyme, saxifrage, granite – a measure
of reassurance there, I felt, and turned
outward again to where the vultures hung
in the shimmering thermals.
                           I had a guide, *Les Oiseaux
des Pyrénées*, with a page of silhouettes,
raptors in flight, identified
by the angle of their wings, the disposition
of pinions and tailfeathers; but the birds outsoared
my eye for detail, indifferent to the constraints
of gravity, nomenclature: *le vautour fauve*,
le gypaète barbu...
                     Was it the unfamiliar
syllables in my mouth, the altitude, a trick
of the astounding light? The world
seemed suddenly charged, pervasive. I could say
some barrier went down; but that's
not it. How shall I put it? There's the intractable
complexity of the fissured rock; the sky
potent, immediate, as if you breathed it in
with the tart smell of the conifers; the birds sustained
at the limits of definition. And if it wasn't
prayer, that elation as I watched them rising
in spirals on the dizzying air until
my vision blurred, I don't know what to call it.

Call

Later I saw her lifted up and passed
over the heads of the swaying crowd, one arm
dangling loose, her inverted face a slack
white mask, her matted hair unbound and tumbling
about her bearers' shoulders; but for the moment
she seemed to stand apart, inviolably
herself – legs braced, her skimpy body moving
to its own rhythms, untroubled by the mob's
blind pulse and swell. Even when she fell
it was with a kind of grace, a decorous
folding at the knees, her neck arched forward,
hands at her sides. And the band,
as you'd expect, played on, the guitars going wild
as she hit the littered floor.
                                        Someone else's
kid, strung out I'd guess
on dope or drink; and someone
else would take the panicky call from wherever
she ended up. But all that night I lay
between sleep and waking, watching her languorous fall
replayed ad nauseam like the grainy footage
of an assassination; or homing in
on detail – a heel
grazing her bangled wrist, her small mouth gasping
or crying out, magenta lipstick smeared
down to the jawline.
                              A little before dawn
the singing began – no, not
singing exactly: a plangent note
unnervingly sustained, and somewhere beneath it
a restless whispering like the sound of parched
maize-stalks pressed together by the wind. Just
noise I might have thought if I hadn't sensed her
close in the unforgiving darkness, smudged
lips working furiously, desperate to get through.

Wargame

I'm reading the instructions. *When you die*
this message will appear on screen: PRESS ANY
KEY TO CONTINUE. *If you wish* –
                                          Our wishes
are neither here nor there. The children lie

in the corridors of hospitals, the dank
cellars of shattered houses. Perhaps some loose
connection? The tears, the bewilderment, the small
white fingers slackening as the screen goes blank.

Sparrowhawk

Thirty years on, the scene's as clear as any
from that phase of my childhood: sunlight falling
on the lawn, the flowerbeds, warming the creamy throat
and belly of next door's tomcat as it drowses
beneath the buddleia; the hawthorn's slender trunk
angled towards the outhouse; a flock of chaffinches
moving among its leaves. I'm sitting
cross-legged, absorbed, watching the bees home in
on the drooping plumes of goldenrod.

                            It's this
I can't lay hold of: lapse of a skipped
heartbeat; a darkening
of the air; a cloud, a shadow; knowledge of space
and silence.

            What follows is the audible
conjunction of flesh and talons as the flock
scatters like shot; the drift of cinnamon
feathers between the branches, shrill cries fading
into distance as the yellow light floods back
across the gardens. But it's on that instant
of suspension the whole thing centres, on the taut
hiatus between ease and panic, breath
and breath, the bill agape, the child's mouth rounded
as though to speak or scream; the cold
premonitory ecstasy stiffening wings and tongue.

Transparency

An idle game: I hold the neat square to the light
and let the winter sun shine through you; or I shift
focus from your translucent features to the twigs
stirring beyond the window

and back again. Late summer; your face half-shaded
by apple-leaves. Above you
and out of view the fruit is being picked
and dropped.
                Caught. In this frame are held

the swirl of skirt and hair, the unbalanced stance,
your laughter as you spin to face the lens
cupping the flawless apple in your palms.

Not all were caught as cleanly. Somewhere, a box
piled high with others, nicked and bruised. I remember
juice on our fingers, skin beneath the nails.

Prospect

Those were, I suppose, the days. I headed northward,
fluent, improvisatory, attuned
to the easy rhythms of the rural
hinterlands where nobody spoke English
and everything made sense. I was travelling
lighter than ever before: a change of clothes,
my shaving kit, a towel, *The Prelude*, tied
in a tattered bedroll. I'd left the map behind
and should have left the razor. My negligence
became a matter of pride, my thickening beard
an emblem of the richer life I'd planned
through childhood and schooltime. Every night,
restless beneath the sliding constellations,
I saw myself where the charted roads give out
striking across the tundra in a haze
of summer light, forehead and cheekbones tanned,
hair streaming in the wind.
                              The route was clearly signed
but I passed the turning, making for the town
and your letter, *poste restante*.

There's something missing. I'm trying to understand
what happened next, how it was I found
myself in the gents up some dark sidestreet, craning
into the pockmarked mirror, razor in hand.

Back

We'd guessed already, of course – pressing between
the unruly hedgerows up lanes whose surface crumbled
beneath our boots; or stumbling
through bracken when the lanes gave out. And yes,
the signs were everywhere – the herds
of feral cattle on the hillsides, tractors
rusting in smothered gateways, the blank
stare of deserted farmsteads; but nothing
spooked us like the choughs, the dark hordes lifting
from the cliffs at our approach to wheel and cry
above our heads. We stood
in the fading light and listened to the breakers
hammering the rocks below us; heard the ousted
spirits sweeping back to claim their own.

Memorial

What was there to remember? Hadn't it always
been like this, the bombsite open
to an unbroken sky, the sun
burning our necks and forearms as we crouched
over jacks or marbles, fought or talked?

                        The long
implausible days unfold again: I'm stumbling
over rubble, hugging a wall whose patterned
paper hangs in rustling strips. I re-examine
the small chipped cup placed on the cellar steps
by whom? If I call
my friends will gather, curious, reaching out
to grasp the equivocal find.

                Even now
these are familiar faces. But who is this boy who stands
a little apart, his eyes averted? Or this girl
advancing gravely from the ruined doorway
a sheaf of fireweed in her blistered arms?

Plenty

The phrase seemed right for the time. *There are*, we'd say,
plenty more fish in the sea. I taste it again, the heady
mixture of greed and insouciance; the future waiting
for what we might care to do to it.

                                        Have I invented
these insistent images? Trawlers strung out across a pale
expanse of sea in stormlight, their brown hulls shrouded
in luminous spray; the wet ropes taut, the seethe and slide
of life plucked from the prodigal waters. Strong hands
guiding the swollen nets; the holds crammed full, the decks
shining with scales. All this
like some grained newsreel, the residual shadow of a world
we loved unwisely.

                            Where shall we go from here,
knowing what we know? Spillage and exploitation, repeated
patterns of violation; soft white bellies turning
to an impassive sky. Our children know it too, the stench
blown from the littered shoreline, the struggle for release
from stifling dreams; the ineluctable roles played out
in rented bedrooms to the scream of gulls, the wind
rattling the casements; the unemployed
haunting the sullen back-streets; the deserted quays.

The Garden

(1916)

I

Damp loam beneath her shins. The currants clustered
above, around her; her mouth is crammed, her hands
stained to the wrist. Framed by the pungent leaves,
one heel scuffing his spade, her father leans
against the enclosing wall. She strains to catch
his murmured words but it's the other's strident
voice comes breaking through: ... *last time I'll tell you,
keep the brat out of here* – her father touching
his cockled hat-brim.

                   It was after that
they started, the dreams of loss, of stilted movement
through luminous spaces, face upturned, mouth venting
a stanchless grief: the child's blind anguish ringing
down the succeeding years.

                      Tonight
thrust back against the water-butt, she hears
her father close the scullery door and shuffle
into the parlour, where the resinous wood
cracks in the grate. Her left hand, fumbling
the whitewashed brick, finds palpable her dreams'
bleak intimations. Inside, the familiar patterns
of sound and shadow; here
this boy's raw love, his searching fingers, sweat
through chafing khaki.

                         Light pouring in; the rank
equivocal odour of the broken leaves.

II

Another world. The lumbering trams, the long
untidy vistas, jostle of rags and furs. The day
oddly disjointed: here her own face staring
(falls of white lace, the brutal mannequins)
from dazzling windows, there the sunlight
gilding the bitter coffee while his fingers
drum on the table; and throughout, this cold
improbable acquiescence.

                                She sees herself ascend
the splintered steps, pass slowly through the dusk
into the shuttered bedroom, indifferent now
to his predatory movements, to the quick
rasp of his breath; and unsurprised,
waking among the twisted sheets, to hear
a girl's voice howling from the adjacent room.

III

Just these: an acrid smoke
cresting the garden wall, the crying plovers, rain
beading his tunic; their quiet, perfunctory loving
in the dank orchard; his clasp-knife
halving the apple, the larva at its core.

IV

At intervals, his letters: he is well,
the weather foul, he loves her still. No code,
no hidden postscript; but her hoarded knowledge
augments the poor smutched phrases.

                                            Again
hunched sleepless on her bed, taking up the sharp
disquieting fragments, images unreal
and vivid as in dreams: the gaitered legs
bruising green barley; a struggling girl pinned down
on the wet floor of a barn; two soldiers
pressed close against a roadside bank, one straining
to hold a shuddering mare, the other groping
with bloodied hands among the hedgerow flowers
and whimpering like a child.

                                    The wind
rattles the sash. Out in the night, the blunt
pencils, the guttering candle-stubs; the abandoned
crying out for ease between the darkening lines.

V

So many leaving now: she sees them stepping
awkward in uniform down sunlit streets or grouped
uncertainly at familiar corners. Edgy
laughter along the towpath, inadequate farewells
on station platforms. Throughout the shortening days
the trains steam southward, heavy with their rich
irreplaceable freight; and households reassemble
around unlaid places, vacant chairs.

                                            The garden
runs to waste. Within the breached
precinct, the fowl are scratching. Beyond, the ungathered
grain, the ripe fruits rotting where they fall.

Schoolfriend

If ever you're passing through... Your invitation
stands, though times have changed. I note
the shadows around your eyes, a surprising
taste for bric-à-brac. An ornate clock
ticks slowly on the mantel. Coals shift and settle
in the guarded grate. Late sunlight slanting
across the polished table, we sit and talk
of nothing in particular while your husband
tidies around us. My wife withdraws
to the next room, where your children
teach ours some game of chance: I hear the dice
skittering across the floorboards.

Night; and I shake
restless between the unfamiliar sheets. What if I take you
home by some other route, skirting the schoolyard, cutting
(you slip your arm through mine) down lanes
whose names elude me? We emerge
into a field long since built over. I dream your breathing
deepening among the grasses, dream the rucked
cloth riding upward from your knees; I follow
your thighs' long contours, pressing forward
into another future. One of the children
cries out. I'm lost. Who is it rises
warm from my side, pads out into the dark?

Vacant Possession

I close the door behind me, pick my way
between mouldering cardboard boxes to the lounge.
Or bedroom: beside the fireplace
a sofa draped with sheets and blankets, pillows
stacked on the floor; a bedside table.

Dusk. The unkempt shrubs
crowding the windows, a spatter of rain. The shadows
reclaim it all – these sagging chairs,
the shrivelled fern, the gramophone, the clutter
on sideboard, sills and bookshelves, debris
of a concluded journey.

Concluded here, the arthritic fingers shuffling
this wad of photographs? Or tracing
through the case's bevelled glass these clouded husks
of butterflies and beetles, their label's childish
non-commital scrawl? *Lewes, August 1912.*

Somewhere beyond the sour
exigencies of this room the downs lie open
to the flawless sky, their grasses seething
with undiscovered life. A whiff
of chloroform; the killing-jar unplugged
by small hands in a blaze of summer light.

Crossing

Fish-stink and diesel, the harbour
just visible, shrouded; the rail
shuddering as we slow; a ragged gull
trailed in our slackening airstream.

It's almost
nothing, you might say, the haze
suddenly thinning, narrow
wings tilting as the breeze
freshens and veers; white
breast-feathers touched with light.

Offerings

I

Nothing will do. Scuffing the leafmould, searching
at the wood's edge for some token of these days
of unexpected sunshine, of enforced
absence. Not this,
nor this. But the chestnut slips
so cleanly from its casing, sleek,
tailed with pale down. I place it (and the gift
grows suddenly unmanageable: this expanse
of frosted grass, the shivering leaves, the sky's
impossible lustre) in your imagined palm.

II

Perhaps. Or it might be this: the redwings gathered
in the berried hedgerow, nettles
and elder against bleached stonework, the play of shadow
on the walnut trunk. Maybe these cups,
delicate, fleshy, bright as coral, scattered
across the woodland floor. And there's no telling:
frost, rot, love, sunlight, this resonant space, the words
tried and found wanting and tried again; again.

Nocturne

Drizzle and darkness falling, so you see it
smudged like a charcoal sketch: the cobbled
thoroughfare gleaming with damp, the cramped perspective
between the leaning tenements, children crowding
the windows on either side. And their lips move
but soundlessly; so you've no idea
whether it's money they want, stretching their ulcered
arms between the bars, their vacant faces
lifted to the invisible stars, or love.

Pain in My Heart

This one again. *Wake up restless nights*
lord and I can't even sleep. Lamplight, the fizz
and crackle of scratched vinyl. Her then,
you now, it's the same old pain, my chest
tight and my heart
stuttering off beat. *I want you to come back*
come back – that plangent southern voice
telling it like it was. Tonight I'm haunted
by a younger self who packs his bags and leaves
to follow a path which, no matter how he breaks
his journey – and I see him on his knees
at the streamside cupping his sunburnt hands or reaching
for a spray of hedgerow berries – leads ineluctably
to this room, this chair, this flawed reprise
of an unrelished past; and by the thought of time
running away like water. Yes, Otis dead
these thirty years and the accumulated damage
of half a lifespan audible in the wash
of background noise. The voice
quieter now, and faltering: *someone stop this*
pain it's pleading as the track fades out.

Appletree

You turn and sigh,
tugging the sheet, and I'm
plucked from my reverie.

Five a.m. and the rain
pelting the windows.
I settle again,

retrace my steps. It's
still where it was, arched
above the blanched grasses, fruits

glowing in sunlight, relic
of an abandoned garden. We
push through the thick

undergrowth, climbing the slope
until we stand in the shadow
of its branches. You stretch up

and forward, your print skirt lifting
behind your knees. The apple
is in your hand. Here nothing

has changed. You extend your arm.
My mouth is open, the white
flesh sweet and warm.

Staying Together

The ladder trembles: a drift of discoloured
vine-leaves loosened on the air; the unsettling
odour of ivy-flowers. Below me
in a dwindling pool of sunlight, you read aloud
just one more story. Ogres
go down like ninepins and the youngest son
comes romping home unscathed to claim
his portion of happiness. If ever after strikes them
as implausible, the children don't let on.

And just one more. One arm between the rungs,
half-hearing the familiar cadences, the phrases
worn thin by repetition, I patch the broken
window-frame. The rusted blade
drags at the putty. Across the gardens
someone is singing, the clear
notes rising light as breath. The sunned
paintwork flakes at my touch; will last
(last year we said the same) another year.

Waiting

Because he turned too late, because he missed
everything but the afterbreath – the twitch and flutter
of the yellowing birch leaves, the hush
as the shaken grasses settled – they couldn't
drag him away but left him out there staring
into the shadows as night came on.

                      He's waited
so long he can hardly move, his back and shoulders
numb as the bole they're pressed against, his eyelids
heavy, his fingers stiff with cold. And there's a lighted
space he can't get back to, a room where others
go about their usual business, bringing
soup to the table, pulling down the blinds.

Pastoral

The scene's not unambiguous. The man
squats with a bucket between his thighs, one hand
on the cow's extended neck, the other
where the hair thickens above her brow. The dry
grasses stir around them. A backdrop
of grey volcanic rock; beyond, a blue
of improbable intensity.
                                        I edge
closer to the window; and as the train
slows on the gradient, I see the creature's lying
on a pad of excrement, her bony haunches
crusted with muck, her flanks caved in, a hindleg
quivering in spasm. There's a pool of shade
cast by a ragged thornbush, but she's stranded
at its hazy margin.
                                Her neck sways suddenly
sideways, but he brings her back, absorbs her
in his own stillness. His face
might be a saint's, shining with concentration
above the grizzled beard. And now
he draws her head – gently, is it, or does he
force her down? – over the bucket's rim. I suppose
she drinks; but as we round the curve, the sun
strikes the grimy glass at such an angle
the whole thing's lost in light.
                                        Well, these are
impoverished lands and perhaps he's simply clinging
grimly to his own livelihood, fingers twisted
in the matted tufts. But I want
to think it tenderness, that questionable pressure
between the upswept horns, I want her held
by love or something like it; and why not standing
where these fields slope to the stream, her forefeet steady
in the pluck and swirl of the current, her running
muzzle lifted to the astounding sky?

Diptych

I

Another birthday; only
everything's muted. She
gazes on distance like
a medieval saint while

the candles slowly
dissolve; waves away
a sliver of cake
a demonstrative grandchild.

She's growing too holy
for food or love. We
can't touch her, can't make
sense of her smile.

II

It's a plausible version
but the cake lies bitten
on the edge of the saucer.
Should the whole thing have been

differently written?
How, though, to ignore
this hunger for heaven?
As the sufferers turn

burning or broken
their faces tilt upward. We
deal as we can
with appetite, pain.

Allowance

Back to the facts: the tight
pink roses nodding in the border, rue
crushed between thumb and finger, the stony light
baffled by foliage. And there's more
of course – ridged stems of hemlock leaning
into the shadows, cacophony
of geese in flight, these beaded lines of silk
strung from the shrubs – but nothing whispering
of luminous ulterior landscapes, nothing
to hint at patterns concealed behind the contours
of what we think we know; only this sharp
uncluttered stringency. Take it or leave it, that's
what's on offer; what the day allows.

Miracle

Who's telling this story, me or you? I said
it was an osprey and so it was, though strangely
pale in colour, lifting above the reedbeds
with a fish clamped in its talons. How should I know
what kind of fish? – a bream perhaps, deep-bellied
certainly, almost a foot in length; but that's
not the important thing. No, what matters,
so far as I'm concerned, is this: as the bird
laboured for height, the fish – and you have to imagine it
twisting from side to side, the sunlight glinting
on its scales, its bony mouth
opening and closing – began to pray: *Ave Maria* –
in Latin, yes, why ever not? and clear
as my own voice now but higher, like a child's,
plaintive, fretful, a little scared.

                              But naturally:
such prayers are always answered. I could see
the wing-beats weakening and then – oh, like a stone,
though of course it didn't sink, but rested a moment
outstretched on the rippled surface. When it rose
the fish was gone. And that's not all: I can't
quite get this straight, but even the bird – I mean
the loss was nothing; you'd know if you'd watched it mounting
suddenly disburdened, its feathers shedding water,
water or light in streaks and flashes, climbing
so steeply you'd have thought – well, what you think's
your own affair; it's all the same to me.

Spring

Everything in excess – the light so bright
he can't stop weeping, all that stir and song
in the thickening hedgerow, bustle
and cluck of the swollen brook, the unendurable
glamour of renewal. Where the path gives out
his slow tread falters. He moves to the gate and leans
a moment on the bar (his wrists as white
as the hazel-switch he peeled in this same copse
almost a lifetime ago while she
bent over him, her fine hair blowing
across his cheek and mouth, making him turn
aside to catch his breath) to catch his breath.

Familiar

Whose is the dog? Padding along behind her,
stopping at intervals to nose the flattened
tussocks beside the footpath, he might be anyone's,
no one's. But when she tries to lose him, striking out
across the sunlit slope towards the birchwood,
he's at her side, a stubborn
indefatigable presence; and they climb together
hugging the beck's mossed edge.

                                    She stoops
cupping her hands; drinks it all in, the icy
water, the ragged skyline and the gleam
of the leaning birches. That cry; the buzzard lifting
from the rocks above her, sliding like a brown
shadow across her vision. Mingled scents
of sheep-dung, gorse, damp turf; but also
some darker undertone.

                        The dog
snuffs the air. And she knows already (fifty
yards upstream the seething flesh, the reddish
bone protruding, matted lumps of fleece
littering the hillside) where he's leading her
and what she'll find; and how he'll trail her home.

Deadline

I'm writing fluently – a straightforward
narrative bridge – when, at the margin
of the road he's taking from A to B, my character
as yet unnamed – I call him X – makes out,
lunging towards him in the headlamps' glare,
a stooping figure, arms across its chest,
clutching a ragged bundle.
                              Closer, I see
the woman's crying out, her features twisted
with rage or pain, her sparse hair whipped
about her hollow cheeks, see how the wind
lifts the damp tatters of her coat; but only
at the last – I mean
as she steps into the road – does it occur to me
that it's a child she's holding, its writhing body
lapped in a threadbare blanket.
                              Does the bumper
clip her as she stumbles? X
has noticed nothing untoward. I keep his
mind on his destination, his hands
firmly on the wheel. I don't look back.

Encounter

I hadn't thought of you for months; but there you were
detaching yourself from the evening crowd, approaching
with the old irresolute smile, impeccably
dressed as ever. You were nervy, eager,
gripping my coatsleeve, swaying a little, wine
and peppermint mingled on your breath. You wanted
to talk. I was busy.
                              I left you standing
unsteadily at the kerbside. As I looked back
you raised your hand in a gesture of dismissal
and resignation, a mocking half-salute.

You knew already, of course; my ignorance
troubles me now. Can I make you out,
so pinched and small, a frail, ambiguous presence
beneath the streetlamp or in the muted glow
of a hushed ward as the night draws in and colour
bleeds from the bedside flowers?
                                          The shadows
thicken around you. Did you hesitate,
fretful, uncertain, before you slipped away
into the bewildering darkness? Was anyone there
to take your arm and see you safely home?

Conjuror

They've kept the best for last. After the games
in the hot green garden, after the brandy-snaps,
the cakes, the ices, the tinted milk, he enters
with his leather suitcase. And he's all smiles
and patter; she sits, hugging her scented knees,
entranced by the mysterious cards, the glasses
turning wine to water, water to wine
till everyone's confused. But it's the hat
she covets: not just the rabbit
(she'd expected that) but all these squares of silk
twitched from its depths, red, yellow, turquoise, pouring
over the buckled brim (but how
could there be so many?) brushing her upturned face,
drifting about her like the petals strewn
at her auntie's wedding. 'And anyone,' he's saying,
'can do it. This little girl...' He reaches down
and takes her hand so that she rises, blushing,
to stand beside him. 'Of course you'll need –' She grasps
the wand. 'And this.' He tucks the hat
beneath her trembling arm. 'Now, when I ask you
to say the magic word –' She blurts it out:
abracadabra.
        His eyes are widening
in mock surprise. 'Oh dear,
oh dear, oh dear, I'm afraid the little lady...
what have we here?' His fingers probe
the dark interior, pulling out clumps
of shredded newsprint, lengths of string; a twisted
stocking, a bone, a set of clacking teeth
dropped like a burning coal to jig and stutter
across the table. The children roar. The hat
seems bottomless. There's nothing she wouldn't give
to recall the untimely word, to stem the issue
of filthy scraps and find herself (it
never happened, it never
happened) once more among the flowering silks.

Whoever

I thought it was you, but it doesn't matter. Whoever
was with me then will remember how the cart-track
narrowed abruptly, choked with brambles, the thorns
tugging at skin and clothing as we struggled
through the untended garden; the yellow tomcat
curled on the sill; the key
beneath the stone as promised.
                              If not yours
whose hands in the evening sunlight cupping their dark
trove of berries, whose forearms
beaded with blood? And whose quiet breathing
at my ear each night, inseparable from the distant
sigh of the breakers?
                      A week? Ten days? – the summer
spent, the berries in the wet
hedgerow bloated, their sweetness gone. I scan
the riddling shadows as though I might catch her turning
one last time on the track as the rain sweeps in
across the shrouded hillside or leaning forward
so that her face comes clear, to say goodbye.

Burning

Yes, burn them all. You meant the lot; and no,
not dumped like refuse. There's an etiquette
informs such matters: letters are burned. I heap
the grate with brittle tinder, jam them in,
still in their envelopes. The flames
climb slowly; the twigs begin to spit and sing.

I've not reread them – all those pages crammed
with thought and afterthought, your nervy script
clotting the margins, breaking out in dense
unruly footnotes. And *let them go*
I might say, *let the whole thing go* – a grand
valedictory gesture; but the stubborn wads
flicker and sulk, hold out against the bright
simplicities of a purgatorial blaze.

What does it matter? But I rake and prod
whatever remains unburned: *and so much more
to say* – the blackened flakes fan out – *since love
can never* – never what? I crane
into the acrid smoke, the tears
prickling behind my eyelids. The cockled scraps
whisper and stir like living things: *across
your face in sleep*, I read, and *are no words*.

Kingfisher

I might have spoken (out there the dazzle
flung from the rippled surface, breaking in stars
and flakes on the leaning alders, on the scarred
stone of the bridge; the bird
skimming away, a spark, a brittle
sliver of turquoise light against the hot
pinks of willowherb and balsam, jinking
at the river's turn; and you
twisted towards me, for the barest instant off-
balance, your own
lips slightly parted) but I let it pass.

The Given

So little to help me place it. I feel the garden
can't have been ours, though my father's there beside me
on the narrow bench: neither the yew
nor the crumbling wall it stands against recurs
in any other context. Early spring
unquestionably, the yew-flowers hanging
in luminous clusters; and my father
reaching across to show me how the pollen
drifts from the shaken branches.
                                    How to understand
that visitation? A flock of – I've always thought
goldfinches, but as I broach the word
I start to doubt it; and surely
not in such numbers? – suddenly around us
as if we'd summoned them from the air, descending
with cries and flickering wingbeats in a wash
of hallucinatory light, the drooping sprays
they brushed against or settled on transmuted
by their fleeting presence.
                                    Yes,
goldfinches. This
is the given; and though I know my father
would never have held me quite so close, his face
warm against mine while the finches swirled and piped
about our heads and the yellow dust went up
in shimmering plumes, what else should I be true to?

Dealing with Circe

After the storms, the freaks, the spells, the roaring
escapades, he's back, filling the space
I'd come to think my own, hogging the ragged
coverlet so the cold airs come and go
across my faded skin. For hours I've watched him
wallowing in uneasy sleep, his head
huge in the dithering lamplight, cheeks and brow
shining with sweat, mouth wide. Smell of the sty.
                                                    He's
not the man he was. Last night, my face
rammed hard against the bedframe while he served me
as a mastiff serves his bitch, I heard him breathe
her name again.
                    This is the only story
I can't get straight: a menagerie
run amok, the sensual current swollen
to an implacable tide, nature herself
upended; and the whole farrago riddled
with evasions, imprecisions. Being protected –
some herb or sorcery, I don't know, the details
vary with the telling – he was never
unfaithful exactly (and whenever he speaks of this
his scarred hand fumbles at his beard, his goggling
eyes flick sideways) but even so, a man
has needs – yes, and regrets, though of course his love
was always here with me and whatever happened
took place without the soul's assent, the body
lapped in its own delirium and confounded
by the sighing darkness.
                        Something like that. I'm sick
of trying to sort it out. I know my place
and it isn't here, spreadeagled in the debris
of someone else's life.
                        He grunts,
stretches an arm towards me. I'm out of bed
and padding through the echoing hall, my soles
tacky with the blood we're still not rid of

for all the servants' scrubbing. I'm going back
to my uncluttered workroom and the scent
of resin entering on the wind. I'll sit
upright at my loom and watch the saffron
light come flooding in, the intricate patterns
sharp in my mind; take up the thread again.

Crop Circles

There's always an explanation. We've heard
from cranks and rationalists, seen how the hoaxers
create their own effects. It's easy: all you need's
a length of rope, a pole, a batten-end.

We know all that. But still the crops are shaken
to their thirsty roots, and still the people gather
in fields at dawn, breathing the irreducible
fragrance of broken wheatstalks, lost for words.